544

201

137
9

46

CO.204

02 2

35

40

8
Co.

11TH

292

24

5

20

111

ENGINE C° 55

MP 8510

F.D. MACK N.Y.   MP 8

5   5

SCHOOL'S OPEN
DRIVE CAREFULLY AAA

FF **PAUL** BEYER   DIV.*01* BATT.*01* UNIT ENG*006*   FF **PETER** BIELFELD   DIV.*06* BATT.*26* UNIT LAD*042*   FF **BRIAN** BILCHER   DIV.*01* BATT.*06* UNIT ENG*033*   FF **CARL** BINI   DIV.SO. BATT.*00* UNIT RES*005*   FF **CHRISTOPHER** BLACKWELL

Publishing

AMERICAN EXPRESS PUBLISHING CORPORATION
NEW YORK, NEW YORK

INTRODUCTION BY
FRANK McCOURT

TEXT BY
TONY HENDRA

BROTHERHOOD

EDITED BY TONY HENDRA   DESIGNED BY MICHAEL IAN KAYE, SOOHYEN PARK, AND BILL DARLING   TYPESET BY NIGEL KENT

DISTRIBUTED BY STERLING PUBLISHING CO., INC.

THIRD EDITION

FF GREG BUCK DIV.08 BATT.40 UNIT ENG 201   CPT WILLIAM BURKE JR DIV.03 BATT.08 UNIT ENG 021   AC DONALD BURNS DIV.AD BATT.OP UNIT CMDCTR   FF JOHN BURNSIDE DIV.01 BATT.02 UNIT LAD 020

CONTRIBUTING PHOTOGRAPHERS

ALEX & LAILA	DAN HALLMAN	PLATON
DAVID BARRY	BRAD HARRIS	PETER RAD
FRITS BERENDS	VISKO HATFIELD	JEFF RIEDEL
CARTER BERG	MELISSA HAYDEN	JEFFREY SCHIFMAN
DAN BIBB	TOM HAYES	KEN SCHLES
MARK BORTHWICK	BLAISE HAYWARD	BASTIENNE SCHMIDT
CHRIS BUCK	GREGORY HEISLER	WILHELM SCHOLZ
MARTHA CAMARILLO	TROY HOUSE	MARK SELIGER
EJ CAMP	KATVAN STUDIOS	CATHERINE SERVEL
BANU CENNETOGLU	JIM KNIGHT	NEAL SLAVIN
JAKE CHESSUM	COLIN LANE	JAMES SMOLKA
CLANG	GERALD LEWIS	JULIANA SOHN
ROBERT CLARK	DANA LIXENBERG	DANIELA STALLINGER
DANNY CLINCH	MARY ELLEN MARK	BRAD STEIN
ROB DELAHANTY	PATRICIA McDONOUGH	ALASTAIR THAIN
GRANT DELIN	MICHEAL McLAUGHLIN	ALBERT WATSON
BRIAN DOBEN	ERIC McNATT	CHRISTIAN WEBER
JASON FULFORD	GREG MILLER	KAI WIECHMANN
DANA GALLAGHER	KATIE MURRAY	STEPHEN WILKES
OBERTO GILI	ERIN PATRICE O'BRIEN	CHRISTIAN WITKIN
XAVIER GUARDANS	MARTIN PARR	JAMES WOJCIK
MARK HALL	BRYCE PINCHAM	ROY ZIPSTEIN

{ vii }

CPT **FRANK** CALLAHAN DIV.*03* BATT.*09* UNIT LAD*035*   FF **MICHAEL** CAMMARATA DIV.*01* BATT.*04* UNIT PROBY   FF **BRIAN** CANNIZZARO DIV.*11* BATT.*32* UNIT LAD*101*   FF **DENNIS** CAREY DIV.SO BATT.*00* UNIT HMC*001*   FF **MICHAEL** CARLO

NO ONE IN CORPORATE AMERICA GOES TO WORK IN THE MORNING THINKING THEY WON'T COME HOME THAT NIGHT. BUT THAT'S EXACTLY WHAT HAPPENED IN THE AMERICAN EXPRESS FAMILY, AS IT HAPPENED IN THOUSANDS OF OTHER FAMILIES IN THE NEW YORK CITY AREA AND AROUND THE WORLD.

OUR HEADQUARTERS IS DIRECTLY ACROSS THE STREET FROM THE WORLD TRADE CENTER. YOU CAN'T GET ANY CLOSER TO GROUND ZERO. AND ON SEPTEMBER 11, ELEVEN OF OUR COLLEAGUES WORKING AT THE WORLD TRADE CENTER LOST THEIR LIVES.

THIS BOOK IS A WAY OF REMEMBERING THE PEOPLE WHO GAVE THEIR LIVES TRYING TO SAVE OUR FRIENDS, OUR COWORKERS, OUR HUSBANDS AND WIVES, OUR BROTHERS AND SISTERS, OUR SONS AND DAUGHTERS, OUR MOMS AND DADS.

FROM ALL OF US AT AMERICAN EXPRESS, THANK YOU.

KENNETH I. CHENAULT

CHAIRMAN & CHIEF EXECUTIVE OFFICER
AMERICAN EXPRESS COMPANY

DEDICATION

THE STREETS OF NEW YORK INSPIRED THE GENESIS of Brotherhood. *It came from the shrines and monuments created to remember the fallen. It came from the spirit of New Yorkers as they rallied behind their heroes.*

Following the attacks of September 11, I walked through Manhattan with my daughters, and we were struck by the amazing outpouring of sentiment reflected in the memorials that could be found on the sidewalks in front of every firehouse in the city. Despite the overwhelming grief that shrouded the city, there was a tremendous outpouring of love. Even the most jaded New Yorker could not pass without slowing down, drawn in by the magnitude of the feelings that spilled across the walkways — the flowers, the candles, the cards, and most of all, the poster~sized photos of those missing and lost.

As we walked from firehouse to firehouse, we began to see the arrangements of flowers and notes and candles as a new kind of street art. It seemed to me that there had to be a way to capture this raw sentiment, this strong visual representation of grief as seen through makeshift shrines, and to document it for posterity.

Brotherhood was created as a tribute to our firefighters. As the idea for the book developed, the volunteers to help make it happen flooded in. There were many, as evidenced by the acknowledgements. The need to do something has taken over nearly everyone in the city. And as creative professionals, we saw this book as our way to give something back and to create something that would continue to give.

We've included in this book all the firehouses that have lost members from their ranks. And in memory of the 343 men who are lost, we've listed their names as a continuing border throughout the pages of this book. We'd like to thank and dedicate this book to those who served to protect us, and those who continue to serve.

RICK BOYKO
CO~PRESIDENT, CHIEF CREATIVE OFFICER
OGILVY & MATHER

{ xi }

FF JAMES COYLE DIV 01 BAT... ROBERT CRAWFORD DIV SC BAT NC UNIT SFTYB1 LT JOHN CHISCL DIV AD BATT TR UNIT HAZMAT BC DENNIS CROSS DIV 11 BATT 57 UNIT BAT05

One of the greatest privileges of being Mayor of the City of New York is working with the brave men and women of our Fire Department. Even before September 11, the actions of New York's Bravest had proven them to be the greatest and had made them the most admired firefighters in the world. Since that terrible day, they have become an international symbol of courage and of the strength of the human spirit.

My connection with the FDNY stretches back to childhood. One of the earliest experiences I remember is my uncle, a firefighter from Brooklyn, being injured when he was thrown from a ladder truck on the way to a fire. My mother took me to visit him almost every day at Kings County Hospital. It was a slow recovery, and he was in pain for much of the time, but I vividly recall his determination to return to the work he loved.

Firefighters have been my heroes from the time I was a little boy.

Now, New York City firefighters are America's heroes.

Before the terrible attack on New York City, firefighters were already among the most loved and admired people in our city. It is easy to understand why. Firefighters are the purest example of love that we have in our society.

{ xv }

MAYOR RUDOLPH W. GIULIANI

It is human instinct to run away from fire. Firefighters train themselves to run toward fire, determined to save the lives of people they may never have met before. When they enter a burning building, they don't stop to ask the race or religion of the people inside. They don't wonder whether a person is rich or poor. They are motivated by a pure and profound love for human life. And it is this spirit that makes our city and our nation great.

There are some people who believe this courage represents the absence of fear. We know that is not true. Firefighters are in most ways ordinary people, but they are capable of extraordinary heroism because they do not let fear determine their actions. Their courage is found in letting their love for human life, their sense of duty and obligation to their fellow human beings, cause them to rise above their own immediate concerns. In doing so, they set an example for all of us. They remind us what each of us can become ~ selfless, courageous, and heroic at the moment when the pressure is greatest. They show us what we are all capable of in the most difficult and dramatic moments of our lives, as well as in smaller moments all along the way.

There are many rewards to being a firefighter ~ the admiration of children and adults, the deep sense of brotherhood that exists within the firehouse. But this respect and camaraderie are a measure of the risks that are involved in this noble profession. Each day, firefighters know that they may be called upon to make the ultimate sacrifice. But before September 11, 2001, the most New York City firefighters lost in a single day was twelve, in a terrible fire in 1966. There is nothing that could have prepared this department, the firefighters, or their families for the loss of 343 of New York's Bravest. We lost some of the very best of the Bravest that day: highly decorated young firefighters, distinguished veterans nearing retirement, present and future leaders of the department. It was, and remains, more than any of us can bear.

Through the many funerals and memorial services that have taken place over the past months, I have tried to give comfort to the families of our fallen heroes by sharing my conviction that not a single firefighter died in vain that terrible day. They were responsible for orchestrating the most successful rescue operation in the history of our nation. They saved twenty~five thousand lives on the morning of September 11. They gave their lives so that others might live. They met the worst of humanity with the best of humanity.

{ xvi }

The New York City firefighters who lost their lives will be remembered among the greatest heroes of American history. Like the brave soldiers who stormed the beaches of Normandy and those who raised the flag over Iwo Jima, our firefighters found themselves on the front lines of a war between freedom and tyranny. They gave their lives defending our liberty. Their example will continue to inspire us and cause us to search for the best in ourselves. The outpouring of love evident in the cards, notes, and flowers placed outside firehouses across our city, as well as in the crowds of people who stood along the West Side Highway cheering on the rescue workers, shows how deeply we have all been affected by their heroism.

There are people who say that our city and nation will never be the same after the events of September 11. I agree. The example of bravery and sacrifice of New York City's firefighters will guide us and make us even better as we face the future. This book is a tribute to their inspirational and indomitable spirit.

The New York City Fire Department is, above all else, a family.

A family of men and women linked by a unique bond and a noble calling: to save lives at whatever cost.

On September 11 we lost three hundred and forty~three members of that family, our brothers, in a savage attack on the heart of our city.

Before this, the total number of those who had given their lives in the line of duty in the entire 136~year history of our department was 752. On September 11, we lost almost half that number in a single terrible morning. Our grief at this loss is overwhelming.

Yet even in the midst of such sadness, we can take comfort in this knowledge: our brothers did not fall in vain. They spent their last moments on earth pursuing their passion, doing what they had sworn to do: saving lives.

I have traveled all over New York City in the aftermath of this tragedy, and one thing has become clear to me: the firefighters' heroism has dramatically increased the size of our Fire Department family. Now it includes all New Yorkers. They have opened their hearts to us~whether it was by lining the streets to hold up messages of encouragement, covering the front of our firehouses with candles and flowers and expressions of sympathy, donating

FIRE COMMISSIONER THOMAS VON ESSEN

money for bereaved families, or simply shaking hands in thanks, offering a kind word of consolation.

Squad 1 in Brooklyn lost nine of its brothers in the World Trade Center collapse~and its fire truck. But it gained a new family member when a young boy walked into its firehouse and handed over his mountain bike to firefighters so they would have some way to get to their next fire.

The sympathy New Yorkers expressed for their fallen brothers touched us all; it touched the nation and the world. The generosity and affection of the people of New York City will help us rise from this tragedy to carry on the legacy of those who fell, stronger and prouder and more united than ever.

We are all one family now.

BROTHERHOOD

WHEN THE LAST FIRE IS QUENCHED AND THE DEVIL IS
DEAD, WHAT WILL BECOME OF OUR FIREFIGHTERS? NO,
THAT'S JUST AN IDLE FANTASY. WE'LL ALWAYS HAVE OUR
FIREFIGHTERS, BECAUSE FIRE IS AN OLD GOD WHO IS WITH
US FOREVER. WE'LL HONOR THE BRAVEST AND TREASURE
THEM RIGHT THERE IN THE FIREHOUSES WE'VE COME TO
REVERE. ✦ AS THE FIRE ENGINE WAILS BY, YOU HOLD YOUR
SMALL CHILD UP TO WAVE, AND THE FIREFIGHTERS WAVE
BACK. ✦ THEY WAVE BACK. ✦ THEY'RE SPEEDING TO WHAT

{ 1 }

FRANK McCOURT

INTRODUCTION

might be injury ∼ or worse ∼ yet they have time and thought for that small hand. You might be the most hardened of New Yorkers, but that always gets to you, the way they wave and smile from the darkness of the cabin or cling to a vehicle with one hand and wave with the other. When that fire engine passes, we all want to wave. It's the noise and color and drama of men and women on a mission, the most urgent of all, the saving of lives.

We pass firehouses all the time, and, if they're not out on a job, we see the men chatting at the door, checking out the ladies passing by, saying hi to everyone. We know there are others inside sleeping, watching television, reading, studying for exams. Firefighters must be the best read of all public servants.

They shop at local supermarkets, and there's something remarkable about these men in helmets and turnout coats discussing the evening meal. You think there's gonna be plain American food on the table that night or that an Italian is seducing Irish palates away from spuds and steak. But no, the men of West 77th Street in Manhattan are discussing Thai chicken curry, and you'd like to be invited.

To see them at the firehouse door and in the supermarket gives you a comforting feeling. They watch the streets and you wonder if there are statistics proving they deter crime in the blocks around them. When they've survived another day of flames and false alarms, most head for leafy suburbs or beyond, to mortgaged houses and children in safe streets.

We sit with the pictures in this book and we're mystified. The book is a requiem for men who went into those doomed towers and never returned. They could have been doing something else. They could have been businessmen, teachers, architects, electricians, but they chose this life where you take hose or axe to fight that old god. You go into the fire, and, as Dennis Smith notes in his classic book, *Report from Engine Co. 82,* you compete for the honor of holding the nob of the hose, the front position closest to the fire. They man a hose that could be a wild animal. They hack and smash and isolate and drown that other wild animal, the old god fire. When you watch their work from the street or on television, you know there's a choreography in their moves, that even with a chief in charge, the firefighter is in there making one crucial decision after another. You can't believe your eyes when you see them moving towards the flames. And that's where they want to be ∼ in there

{ 2 }

with the action. They move up in the ranks ~ lieutenant, captain, chief ~ yet they don't just stand in the street shouting orders. They're hip to hip with the firefighters wielding axes, with the men on the hose.

We're civilians and we wonder now about the men in the pictures, what they're thinking and feeling, what they're saying to each other away from the firehouse door. If you stop to chat they're pleasant ~ unless you touch on September 11. Then you sense a withdrawal, as if you'd encroached on a family matter.

It just won't be the same anymore when that fire engine passes and we lift the small child to wave. It won't be that simple, and that's because a new consciousness has been raised. Now we'll make eye contact and nod as if to acknowledge that "a terrible beauty" has been born.

You can't merely walk past a firehouse now. You have to slow down, show respect. They've been turned into shrines, and we know why. If we don't have the comfort of church, synagogue, or mosque, we need a place to lay our grief.

Or we have the pictures. Here are the firefighters themselves ~ the living and the dead. There are heartbreaking geometries of helmets, turnout coats, and boots. Oh, any page you turn in this book can break your heart ~ unless you take comfort from those arrangements of candles, flowers, mementoes, declarations of love.

In one picture, up in the left-hand corner, there is a drawing by a third~grader where a firefighter is being asked for his autograph by a trinity of superheroes: Spiderman, Batman, Superman.

We don't have to go to the movies anymore for our heroes. We don't have to turn on the television. Our heroes are down the street, chatting at the firehouse door, ready to face the old god.

{ 3 }

WHEREVER THEY ARE IN THE CITY, IN CENTURY~OLD BUILDINGS OR FLUSH WITH THE MARBLE MASS OF THE LATEST MIDTOWN HIGH~RISE OR HARDY SURVIVORS IN A MOONSCAPE OF EMPTY LOTS, FIREHOUSES HAVE A QUALITY THAT FASCINATES US, THAT DRAWS US TO THEM. THERE ARE 221 OF THEM IN THE FIVE BOROUGHS, AND THEY REFLECT BETTER THAN ANY OTHER INSTITUTION THE ENDLESS VARIETY OF A GREAT CITY, THE MYRIAD CULTURES AND NEIGHBORHOODS OF THE PEOPLE THEY PROTECT. WHILE NO TWO LOOK QUITE THE SAME, ALL HAVE THAT BROODING AURA OF PRIDE AND STRENGTH, A CERTAIN CALM, THE QUIET EXPECTATION OF IMPENDING DANGER. WE FEEL A SLIGHT SENSE OF MYSTERY, EVEN APPREHENSION, AS WE GAZE INTO THEM. FOR ALL THEIR APPROACHABILITY, THESE PLACES ARE APART, SPECIAL; THEY HAVE A MISSION. ✦ THE FIREHOUSES DEPICTED IN THE FOLLOWING PAGES ARE EVEN MORE SPECIAL, SET APART BY TRAGEDY. THEY ARE THE FIREHOUSES THAT LOST ONE OR MORE OF THEIR BROTHERS ON A BRIGHT SEPTEMBER MORNING IN THE YEAR 2001. ✦ THESE ARE THE PLACES WHERE BOUNDLESS COURAGE AND SELFLESSNESS WERE NURTURED. THESE ARE THE PLACES WHERE HEROES WERE MADE.

{ 5 }

THE PLACES

ENGINE COMPANY 5

DANIEL SUHR DIV.11 BATT.35 UNIT ENG216   LT CHRISTOPHER SULLIVAN   DIV.15 BATT.37 UNIT LAD111   FF BRIAN SWEENEY   DIV.50 BATT.00 UNIT SQD288   FF SEAN TALLON   DIV.01 BATT.01 UNIT LAD010

ENGINE 54
LADDER 4
BATTALION 9

FF ALLAN TARASIEWICZ   FF PAUL TEGTMEIER   FF JOHN TIERNEY   FF JOHN TIPPING II   FF HECTOR TIRADO

ENGINE CO. 165
LADDER CO. 85

FF JOSEPH AGNELLO DIV. 11 BATT. 32 UNIT LAD118   LT BRIAN AHEARN DIV. 11 BATT. 57 UNIT ENG230   FF ERIC ALLEN DIV. SO BATT. 00 UNIT SQD018   FF RICHARD ALLEN DIV. 01 BATT. 01 UNIT PROBY   BC JAMES AMAT

LT STEVEN BATES DIV 11 BATT 57 UNIT ENG 235 FF CARL BEDIGIAN DIV 15 BATT 37 UNIT ENG 214 FF STEPHEN BELSON DIV 01 BATT 07 UNIT LAD 024 FF JOHN BERGIN DIV SO BATT 00 UNIT RES 005 FF PAUL BEYE

ENGINE CO. 240   BATT. 48

MICHAEL CAWLEY DIV.14 BATT.46 UNIT LAD136 FF VERNON CHERRY DIV.11 BATT.32 UNIT LAD118 FF NICHOLAS CHIOFALO DIV.11 BATT.57 UNIT ENG235 FF JOHN CHIPURA DIV.11 BATT.57 UNIT ENG219

MICHAEL ELFERIS DIV.03 BATT.10 UNIT ENG022 FF FRANCIS ESPOSITO DIV.1 BATT.57 UNIT ENG235 LT MICHAEL ESPOSITO DIV.SO BATT.00 UNIT SQD001 FF ROBERT EVANS DIV.01 BATT.06 UNIT ENG033

NOWHERE IS LONELIER THAN A PLACE THAT HAS LOST THOSE WHO LIVED IN IT. EVERYDAY THINGS ~ TOOLS, FURNITURE, CLOTHING, QUIET NOOKS, FAVORITE MUGS, PERSONAL TOUCHES ~ THAT HAVE BARELY REGISTERED ON THE CONSCIOUSNESS FOR YEARS SUDDENLY TAKE ON A TERRIBLE MEANING. IMPOSSIBLE NOT TO PROJECT THE LOST ONE INTO THEM, SITTING IN THE CHAIR HE DEFENDED AGAINST ALL COMERS, SHRUGGING ON THAT JACKET IN THAT CERTAIN WAY, SPORTING THAT HEADGEAR AT THAT CERTAIN ANGLE.... ✦ EVERYDAY THINGS IN A FIREHOUSE ~ HELMETS, BUNKER GEAR, BOOTS, A WORKOUT AREA, A CARD TABLE, A ROW OF BEDS, FIRE POLES ~ HAVE AN ADDITIONAL LAYER OF MEANING. THEY UNDERLINE THAT THE FIREFIGHTER'S JOB IS MOSTLY WAITING, ALWAYS LIVING IN AN EDGY STATE OF READINESS FOR UNKNOWN PERILS. ✦ IN TIMES OF TRAGEDY, EVERYDAY THINGS BECOME MUTE MEMORIALS. THEY HAVE AN AWFUL STILLNESS TO THEM, AS THEY NOW WAIT ~ FOR PEOPLE WHO WILL NEVER COME.

{ 89 }

AT HOME

FF SEAN HANLEY DIV 01 BATT 02 UNIT LAD 020   FF THOMAS HANNAFIN DIV 01 BATT 02 UNIT LAD 005   FF DANA HANNON DIV 01 BATT 07 UNIT ENG 026   FF DANIEL HARLIN DIV 03 BATT 08 UNIT LAD

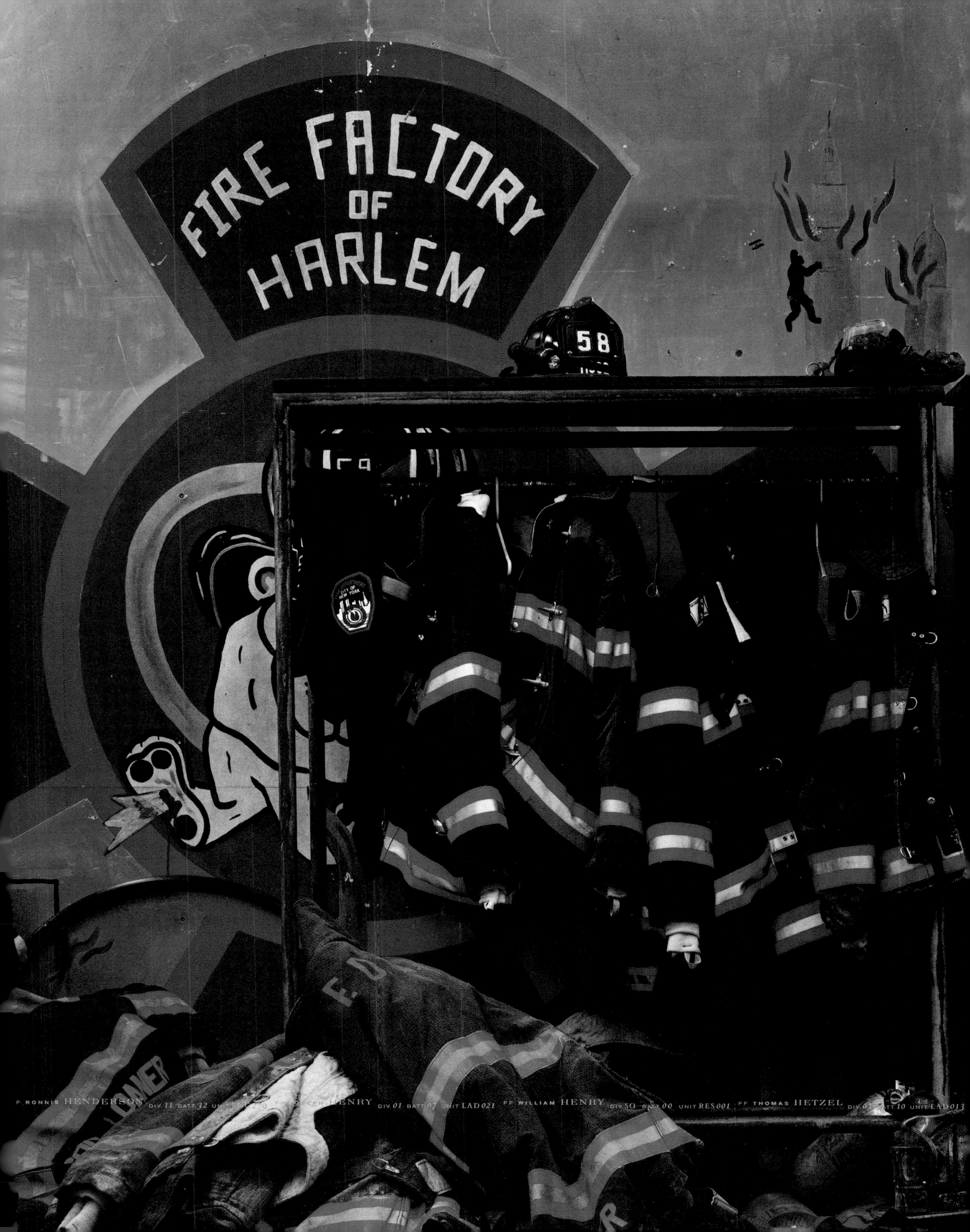
FIRE FACTORY
OF
HARLEM
58

F RONNIE HENDERSON DIV 11 BATT 32 UNIT ENG 279 FF JOSEPH HENRY DIV 01 BATT 07 UNIT LAD 021 FF WILLIAM HENRY DIV SO BATT 00 UNIT RES 001 FF THOMAS HETZEL DIV 03 BATT 10 UNIT LAD 013

ATRICK LYONS   FF JOSEPH MAFFEO   FF WILLIAM MAHONEY

FLOWMASTER

Gallons Per Minute

X 100   TOTAL   CAL.

FLOWMASTER

Gallons Per Minute

X 100   TOTAL   CAL.

FLOWMASTER

Gallons Per Minute

X 100   TOTAL

IDLE

PRESET   PRO
GOVERNOR

SETTING

PRESSURE   RPM

3

NO. 5
2 1/2" DISCHARGE

NO. 2
2 1/2" DISCHARGE

NO. 3
2 1/2" DISCHARGE

DELUGE GUN

NO. 1 FRONT
2 1/2" DISCH

FRONT DISCHARGE

NO. 3
2 1/2" DISCHARGE

DELUGE GUN

IN
CLOSED

Waterous

CLOSE

Waterous

SEAGRAVE FIRE APP., INC.	PERFORMANCE		
105 E. 12TH STREET	5/22/97		
CLINTONVILLE, WI 54929	G.P.M.	PRESSURE	ENGINE RPM
PRODUCTION NO. 91620	1008	160 PSI	1340
PUMP MANUFACTURE WATEROUS	806	200 PSI	1460

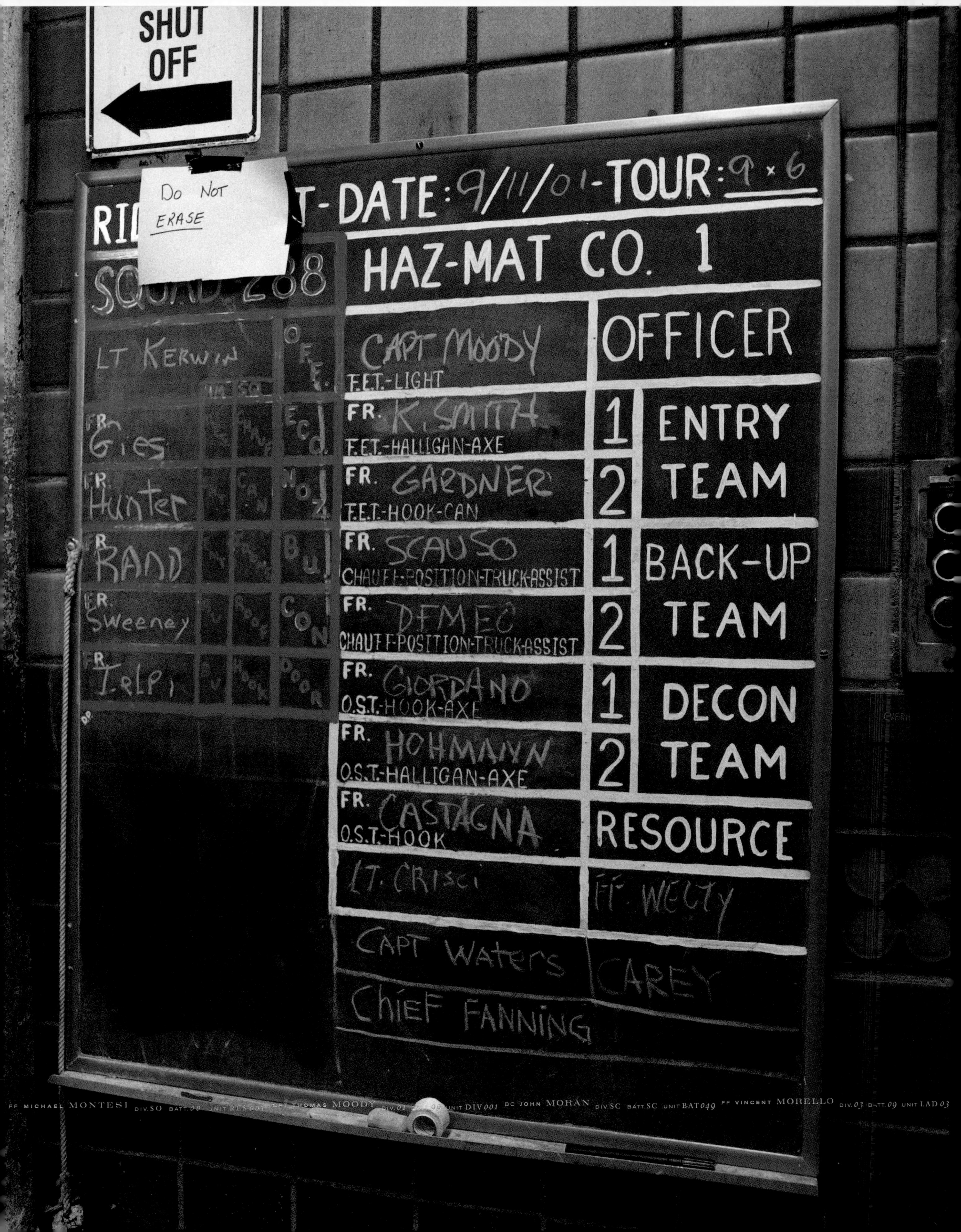
SHUT OFF
DO NOT ERASE
RI… T-DATE: 9/11/01-TOUR: 9 x 6
SQUAD 288
HAZ-MAT CO. 1
LT KERWIN
OFF.
FR. Gies
FR. Hunter
FR. RAND
FR. Sweeney
FR. Ielpi
ECC.
NOZ.
CON
DOOR
HOOK
ROOF
CAN
CAPT MOODY
F.E.T.-LIGHT
OFFICER
FR. K. SMITH
F.E.T.-HALLIGAN-AXE
FR. GARDNER
F.E.T.-HOOK-CAN
1
2
ENTRY TEAM
FR. SCAUSO
CHAUFF-POSITION-TRUCK-ASSIST
FR. DEMEO
CHAUFF-POSITION-TRUCK-ASSIST
1
2
BACK-UP TEAM
FR. GIORDANO
O.S.T.-HOOK-AXE
FR. HOHMANN
O.S.T.-HALLIGAN-AXE
1
2
DECON TEAM
FR. CASTAGNA
O.S.T.-HOOK
RESOURCE
LT. CRISCI
FF. WELTY
CAPT Waters
CAREY
Chief FANNING

FF MICHAEL MONTESI DIV.SO BATT.00 UNIT RES 001 CPT THOMAS MOODY DIV.01 BATT.99 UNIT DIV 001 BC JOHN MORAN DIV.SC BATT.SC UNIT BAT 049 FF VINCENT MORELLO DIV.03 BATT.09 UNIT LAD 03

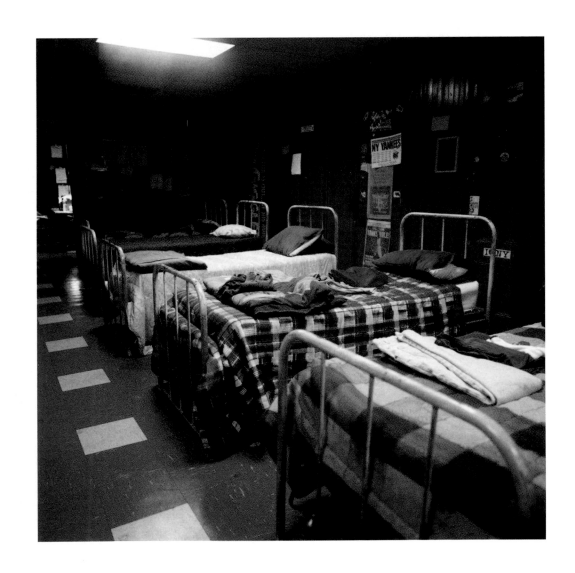

08 BATT. 40 UNIT ENG 201 FF SHAWN POWELL DIV. 1 BATT. 31 UNIT ENG 207 FF VINCENT PRINCIOTTA DIV 03 BATT 08 UNIT LAD 037 FF KEVIN PRIOR DIV 50 BATT

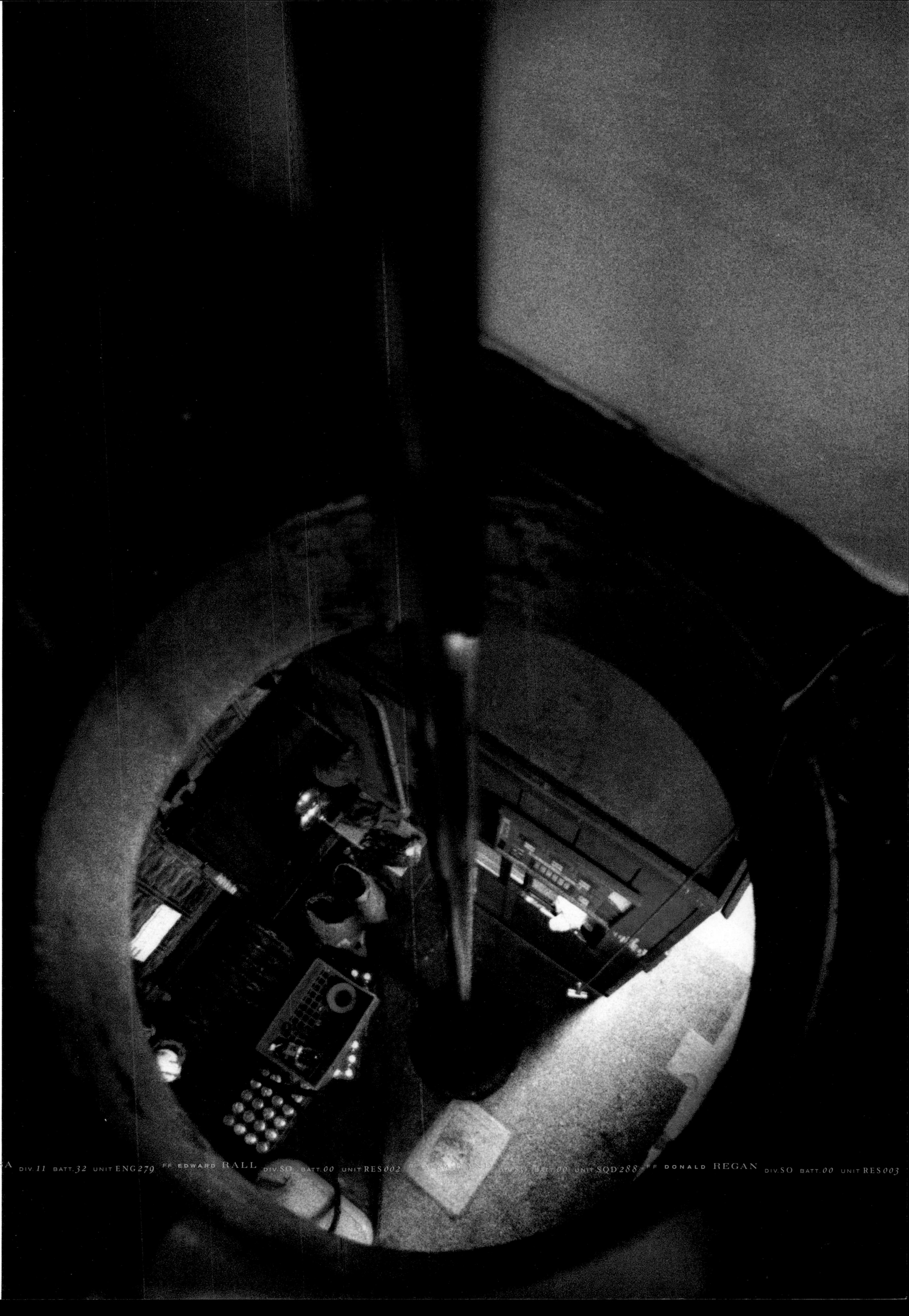

FF MICHAEL RAGUSA DIV. 11 BATT. 32 UNIT ENG 279 FF EDWARD RALL DIV. SO BATT. 00 UNIT RES 002 FF ADAM RAND DIV. SO BATT. 00 UNIT SQD 288 FF DONALD REGAN DIV. SO BATT. 00 UNIT RES 003

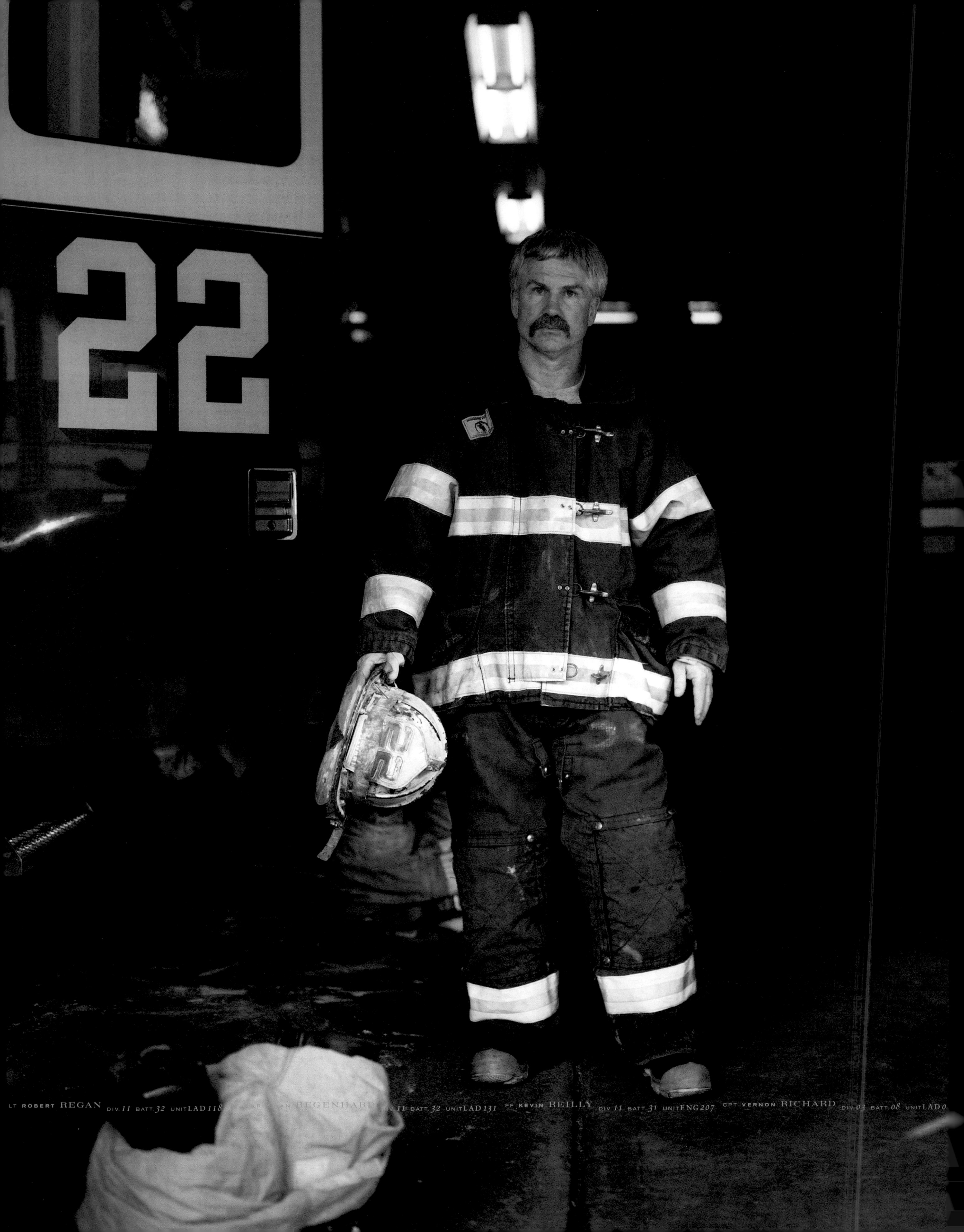

LT ROBERT REGAN DIV. 11 BATT. 32 UNIT LAD 118 FF CHRISTIAN REGENHARD DIV. 11 BATT. 32 UNIT LAD 131 FF KEVIN REILLY DIV. 11 BATT. 31 UNIT ENG 207 CPT VERNON RICHARD DIV. 03 BATT. 08 UNIT LAD 0

THE BROTHERHOOD TO WHICH ALL FIREFIGHTERS BELONG HAS THE HARDEST JOB OF ALL ∼ TO LIVE WITH THE LOSS OF THEIR FALLEN. ✦ FOR BROTHERHOOD IS A TWO∼EDGED SWORD; IT'S THOSE VERY BONDS, SO CLOSE AND CARING, THAT MAKE THE HURT SO BAD. IF EVEN ONE OF THEIR NUMBER FALLS, THOUSANDS FEEL IT AS A PERSONAL LOSS AND HUNDREDS WILL TURN OUT FOR THE FUNERAL. IMAGINE THE PAIN WHEN HUNDREDS FALL. ✦ BUT THEY HAVE THIS STRENGTH TO DRAW ON. YOU CAN SEE IT IN THEIR EYES. IF BROTHERHOOD HURTS, IT ALSO HEALS. BECAUSE ABOVE ALL, BROTHERHOOD ENDURES. IT HAS, FOR ALMOST ONE HUNDRED AND FIFTY YEARS AND WILL FOR HUNDREDS YET TO COME, FACING DOWN THE INCONCEIVABLE AND THE UNIMAGINABLE, DENYING VICTORY TO DESPAIR, STRONG IN THE KNOWLEDGE THAT THIS, TOO, SHALL PASS.

{ 125 }

THE LIVING

FF **CHRISTOPHER** SANTORA *DIV.03* BATT.*09* UNIT *ENG.054* FF **JOHN** SANTORE *DIV.01* BATT.*02* UNIT *LAD.005* FF **GREGORY** SAUCEDO *DIV.01* BATT.*02* UNIT *LAD.005* FF **DENNIS** SCAUSO *DIV.SO* BATT.*00* UNIT *HMC.0C*

SALVATORE CALABRO DIV.11 BATT.32 UNIT LAD 101   CPT FRANK CALLAHAN DIV.03 BATT.09 UNIT LAD 035   FF MICHAEL CAMMARATA DIV.01 BATT.04 UNIT PROBY   FF BRIAN CANNIZZARO DIV.11 BATT.32 UNIT LAD 101

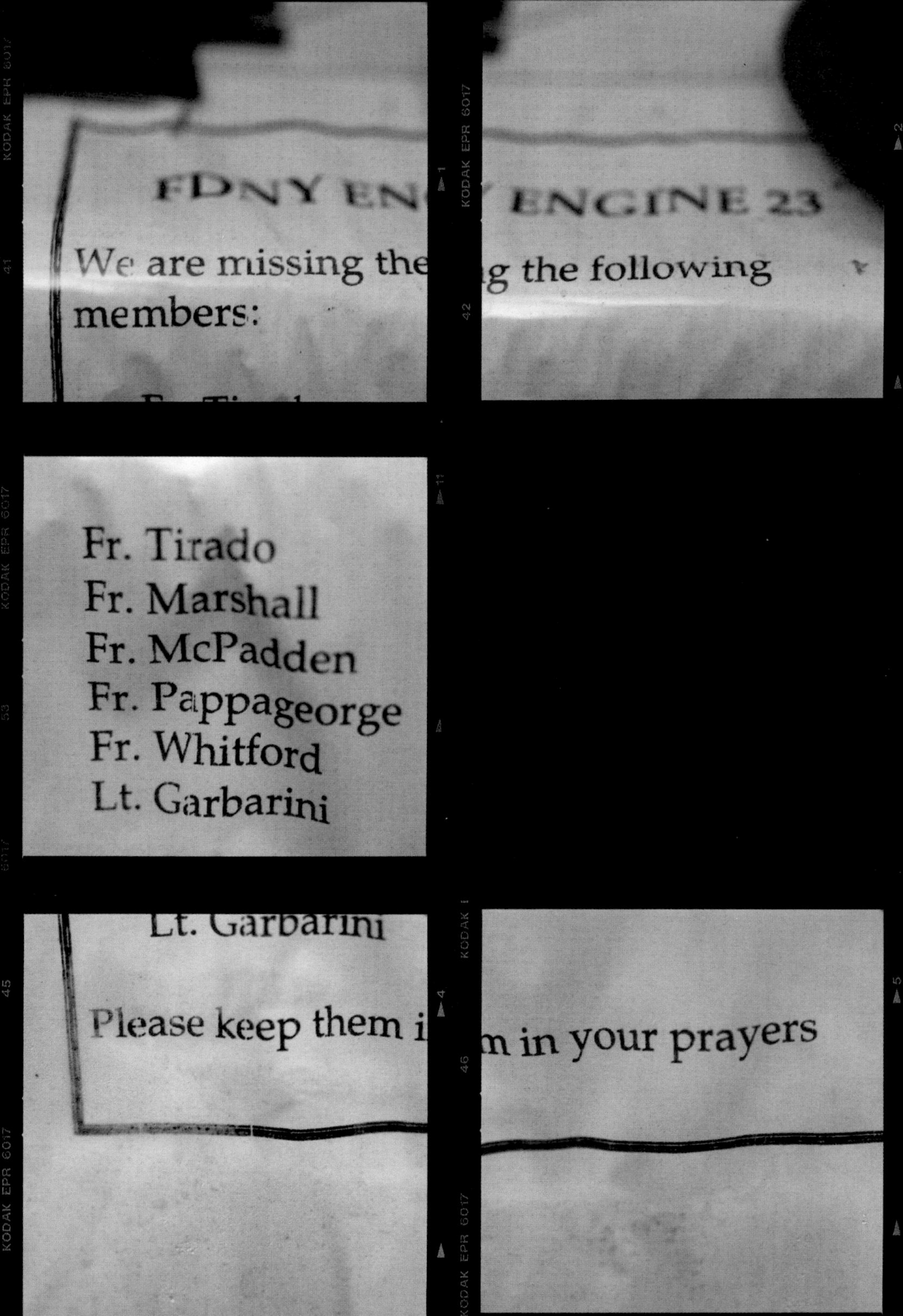

FDNY ENGINE 23

We are missing the following members:

Fr. Tirado
Fr. Marshall
Fr. McPadden
Fr. Pappageorge
Fr. Whitford
Lt. Garbarini

Please keep them in your prayers

IT'S THE CUSTOM OF MANY FIRE DEPARTMENTS, AT THE FUNERALS OF FALLEN FIREFIGHTERS, TO HAVE THEM PLAYED TO THEIR REST BY BAGPIPERS. ✦ SUNDAY AFTER THE HORROR, BESIDE A HUDSON RUBY~RED IN THE SETTING SUN, AS NEAR TO THE RUINS AS HE COULD GET, A LONE PIPER WAS PLAYING. ✦ HE HAD NO CONNECTION TO THE NEW YORK FIRE DEPARTMENT; HE WASN'T EVEN FROM NEW YORK. HE WAS A GUY FROM BOSTON, A PLUMBER BY TRADE, WHO HAPPENED TO BE A BAGPIPER AND HAD BEEN MOVED TO TEARS BY THE HEROISM AND SELF~SACRIFICE OF OUR FIREFIGHTERS. SO HE'D COME TO PAY HIS RESPECTS. ✦ AT THAT TIME THE EXACT NUMBER OF FALLEN WASN'T YET KNOWN, BUT IT WAS PUT AT ABOUT 300. THE PIPER WAS PLAYING A MINUTE OR SO FOR EACH MAN, TRYING TO KEEP EACH TRIBUTE A LITTLE DIFFERENT; PLANGENT RIFFS ON OLD SCOTTISH AND IRISH BALLADS, SONGS OF LOST LOVE AND THE DEATH OF HEROES AND THE LONGING FOR HOME. ✦ HE'D BEEN PLAYING FOR SIX AND A HALF HOURS. BUT EACH LAMENT WAS SWEETER AND MORE HAUNTING THAN THE LAST.

{ 153 }

THE FALLEN

OUR HEARTS
GO OUT TO
ALL, AND
ALL YOUR
FAMILIES.
GOD BLESS
USA &
THANKS FOR
ALL THE HELP
AND LOVE
ALL YOU GUYS
HAVE
GIVEN THE
COMMUNITY
ALL THESE
YEARS AND
THANKS FOR
ALL THE EFFORTS
YOUVE GIVEN
TO THE WTC
ATTACK. WE LOVE
YOU ALL...
GOD BLESS
ALWAYS AND FOREVER
REST IN PEACE.
JUDY. @ 1370 5ᵗʰ

PLEASE PRAY FOR ALL
THE MISSING FIREFIGHTERS
AND THEIR FAMILIES ...
ESPECIALLY OUR DEAREST
FIREFACTORY FAMILY
MEMBERS:
LT. ROBERT NAGEL
AND
FF. TEDDY WHITE

LT. ROBERT NAGEL
HAS BEEN A MEMBER OF
THE F.D.N.Y. SINCE 11/24/73
HE HAS BEEN A FAITHFUL
SERVANT TO THIS HARLEM
COMMUNITY AND
FIREFACTORY MEMBER
FOR OVER 11 YEARS
YEARS

PLEASE PRAY FOR OUR FORMER
FIREFACTORY FAMILY MEMBERS
WHOM ARE MISSING AND
THEIR FAMILIES :
JACK FANNING
PADDY BROWN
TOMMY O'HAGEN

AUTION
ALARM BELL SOUNDS
OIL TANK FILLED TO CAPACITY
DO NOT OVERFILL
PREFERRED UTILITIES MFG. CORP. PA-5

GID BLESS

THA

NOT

LOST BUT
NOT FORG

GOD BE WIT
YOU

PRAY FOR OUR BROTHERS

CAPT.	BRIAN HICKEY	R4	FF. DURRELL PEARSALL	R4
LT.	KEVIN DOWDELL	R4	FF. PETE BRENNAN
FF.	TERRY FARRELL	R4	FF. AL TARASIEWICZ
FF.	BILL MAHONEY	R4	FF. MIKE CAWLEY
FF.	PETE NELSON	R4	

Battalion Chief

Matthew L. Ryan

5-7"   180 LBS.

YOU WILL NEVER BE FORGOTTEN FATHER MYCHAL
REST IN GOD'S PEACE

PRAY FOR OUR MISSING BROTHERS

SL

AUTION

ALARM BELL SOUNDS

NK FILLED TO CAPACITY

DO NOT OVERFILL

FF Joseph Maloney

FF Timothy McSweeney

FF Michael Carroll

FF John McAvoy

Lt. Kevin Donnelly

Battalion Chief John Williamson

FF Jeffrey Giordano

Captain Patrick Brown

FF James Coyle

FF Steven Olson

FF Joseph Capeto

FF Gerard Dewan

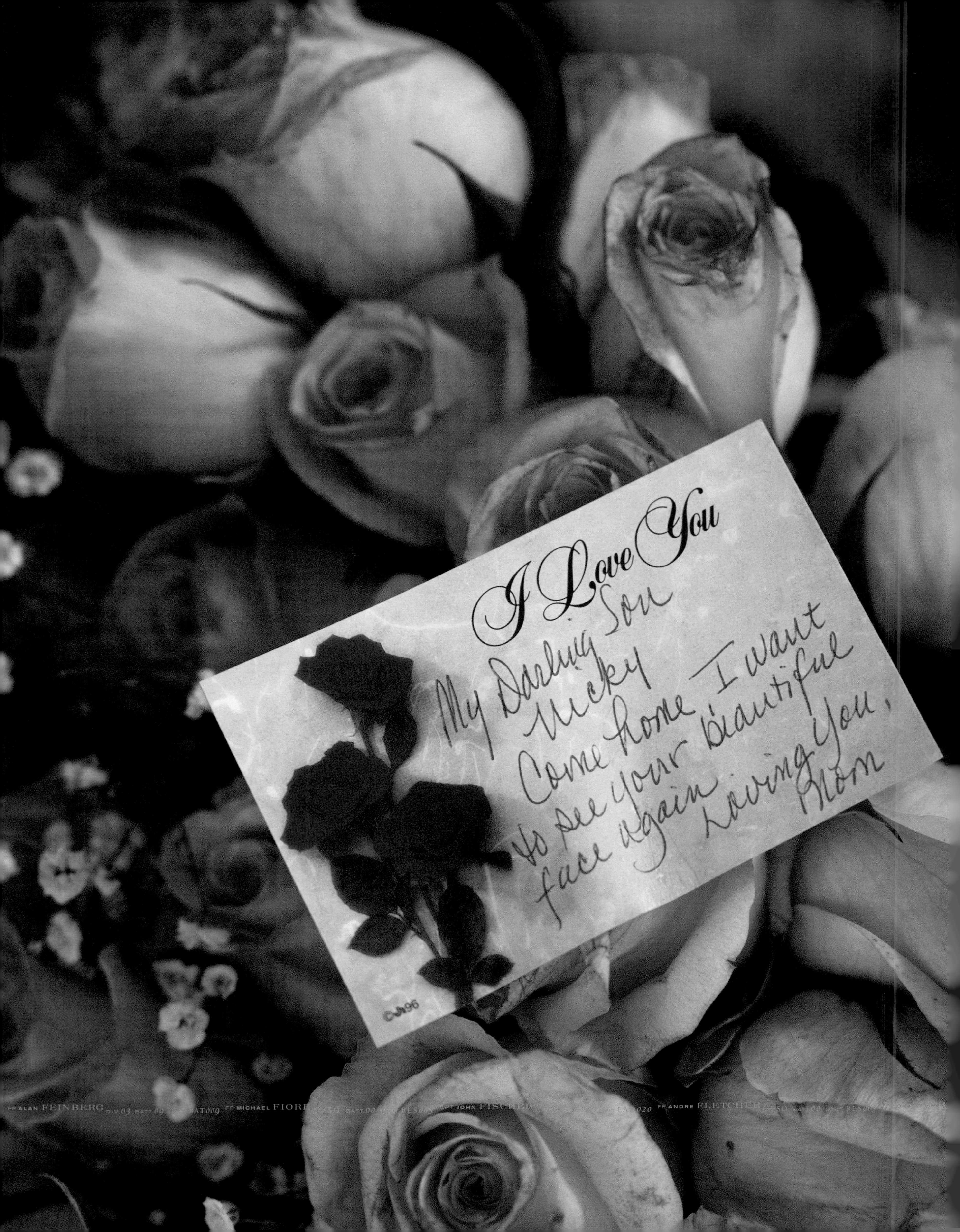
I Love You
My Darling Son
Micky
Come home I want
to see your biautiful
face again Loving You,
Mom
©JN96

FF ALAN FEINBERG DIV 03 BATT 09 ... BAT009 FF MICHAEL FIORE ... BATT 00 ... RES 005 CPT JOHN FISCHER ... LAD 020 FF ANDRE FLETCHER ... BATT 00 UNIT RES 005

Rescue workers,
hank you for
g there for
rica. We know
you had to leave
families to help,
se stay safe and

IS2 (Staten Island)
We're sorry for
rescue workers,
for survivors of
ood luck and
Sincerely
The 6th graders of IS2:

In Sympathy
on your unexpected
and tragic loss.

Chief of Department Peter Ganci, left, with C

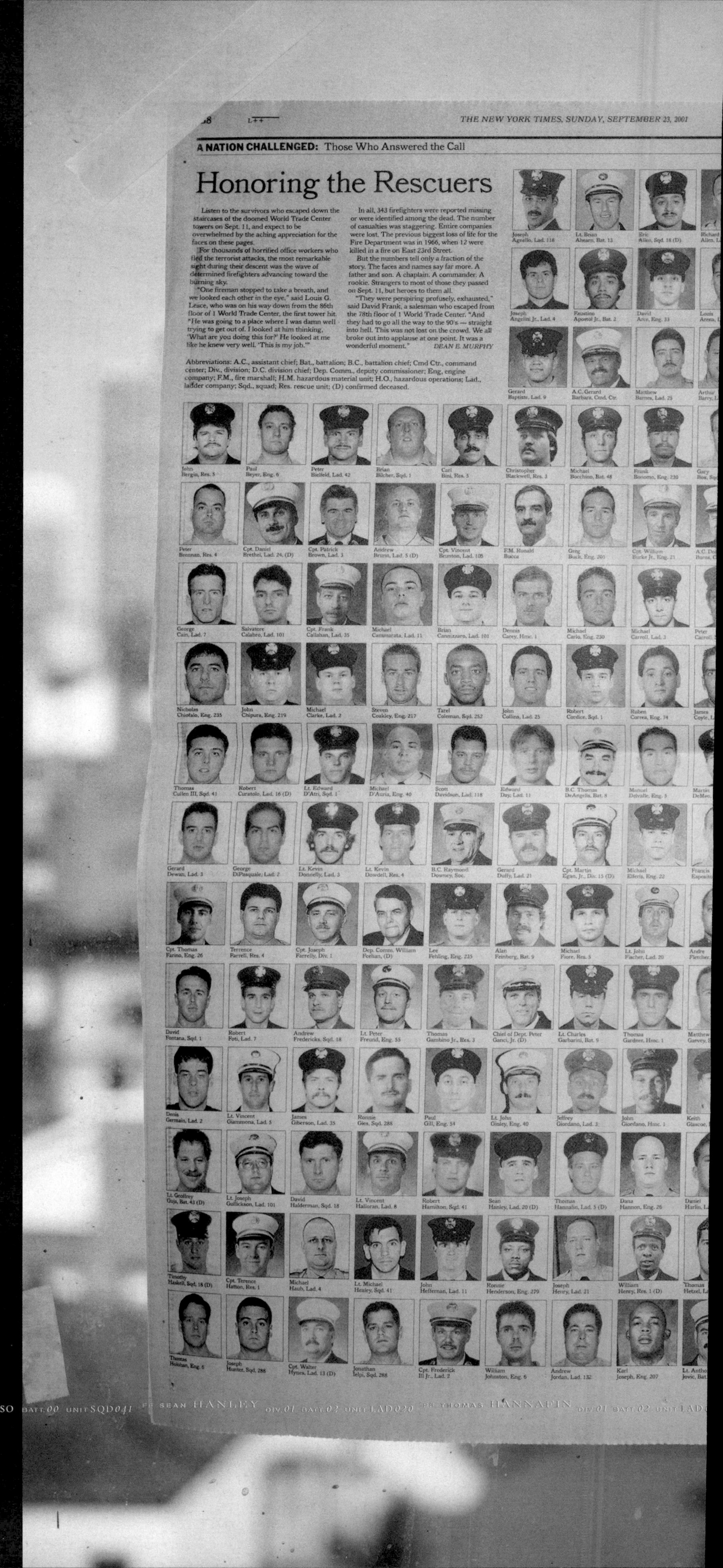

A NATION CHALLENGED: Those Who Answered the Call

Honoring the Rescuers

Listen to the survivors who escaped down the staircases of the doomed World Trade Center towers on Sept. 11, and expect to be overwhelmed by the aching appreciation for the faces on these pages.

For thousands of horrified office workers who fled the terrorist attacks, the most remarkable sight during their descent was the wave of determined firefighters advancing toward the burning sky.

"One fireman stopped to take a breath, and we looked each other in the eye," said Louis G. Lesce, who was on his way down from the 86th floor of 1 World Trade Center, the first tower hit. "He was going to a place where I was damn well trying to get out of. I looked at him thinking, 'What are you doing this for?' He looked at me like he knew very well. 'This is my job.'"

In all, 343 firefighters were reported missing or were identified among the dead. The number of casualties was staggering. Entire companies were lost. The previous biggest loss of life for the Fire Department was in 1966, when 12 were killed in a fire on East 23rd Street.

But the numbers tell only a fraction of the story. The faces and names say far more. A father and son. A chaplain. A commander. A rookie. Strangers to most of those they passed on Sept. 11, but heroes to them all.

"They were perspiring profusely, exhausted," said David Frank, a salesman who escaped from the 78th floor of 1 World Trade Center. "And they had to go all the way to the 90's — straight into hell. This was not lost on the crowd. We all broke out into applause at one point. It was a wonderful moment." *DEAN E. MURPHY*

Abbreviations: A.C., assistant chief; Bat., battalion; B.C., battalion chief; Cmd Ctr., command center; Div., division; D.C. division chief; Dep. Comm., deputy commissioner; Eng, engine company; F.M., fire marshall; H.M. hazardous material unit; H.O., hazardous operations; Lad., ladder company; Sqd., squad; Res. rescue unit; (D) confirmed deceased.

Joseph Agnello, Lad. 118
Lt. Brian Ahearn, Bat. 13
Eric Allen, Sqd. 18 (D)
Richard Allen, L

Joseph Angelini Jr., Lad. 4
Faustino Apostol Jr., Bat. 2
David Arce, Eng. 33
Louis Arena, L

Gerard Baptiste, Lad. 9
A.C. Gerard Barbara, Cmd. Ctr.
Matthew Barnes, Lad. 25
Arthur Barry, L

John Bergin, Res. 5
Paul Beyer, Eng. 6
Peter Bielfeld, Lad. 42
Brian Bilcher, Sqd. 1
Carl Bini, Res. 5
Christopher Blackwell, Res. 3
Michael Bocchino, Bat. 48
Frank Bonomo, Eng. 230
Gary Box, Sq

Peter Brennan, Res. 4
Cpt. Daniel Brethel, Lad. 24, (D)
Cpt. Patrick Brown, Lad. 3
Andrew Brunn, Lad. 5 (D)
Cpt. Vincent Brunton, Lad. 105
F.M. Ronald Bucca
Greg Buck, Eng. 201
Cpt. William Burke Jr., Eng. 21
A.C. Do Burns, C

George Cain, Lad. 7
Salvatore Calabro, Lad. 101
Cpt. Frank Callahan, Lad. 35
Michael Cammarata, Lad. 11
Brian Cannizzaro, Lad. 101
Dennis Carey, Hmc. 1
Michael Carlo, Eng. 230
Michael Carroll, Lad. 3
Peter Carroll, S

Nicholas Chiofalo, Eng. 235
John Chipura, Eng. 219
Michael Clarke, Lad. 2
Steven Coakley, Eng. 217
Tarel Coleman, Sqd. 252
John Collins, Lad. 25
Robert Cordice, Sqd. 1
Ruben Correa, Eng. 74
James Coyle, L

Thomas Cullen III, Sqd. 41
Robert Curatolo, Lad. 16 (D)
Lt. Edward D'Atri, Sqd. 1
Michael D'Auria, Eng. 40
Scott Davidson, Lad. 118
Edward Day, Lad. 11
B.C. Thomas DeAngelis, Bat. 8
Manuel Delvalle, Eng. 5
Martin DeMeo,

Gerard Dewan, Lad. 3
George DiPasquale, Lad. 2
Lt. Kevin Donnelly, Lad. 3
Lt. Kevin Dowdell, Res. 4
B.C. Raymond Downey, Soc.
Gerard Duffy, Lad. 21
Cpt. Martin Egan, Jr., Div. 15 (D)
Michael Elferis, Eng. 22
Francis Esposito

Cpt. Thomas Farino, Eng. 26
Terrence Farrell, Res. 4
Cpt. Joseph Farrelly, Div. 1
Dep. Comm. William Feehan, (D)
Lee Fehling, Eng. 235
Alan Feinberg, Bat. 9
Michael Fiore, Res. 5
Lt. John Fischer, Lad. 20
Andre Fletcher,

David Fontana, Sqd. 1
Robert Foti, Lad. 7
Andrew Fredericks, Sqd. 18
Lt. Peter Freund, Eng. 55
Thomas Gambino Jr., Res. 3
Chief of Dept. Peter Ganci, Jr. (D)
Lt. Charles Garbarini, Bat. 9
Thomas Gardner, Hmc. 1
Matthew Garvey, S

Denis Germain, Lad. 2
Lt. Vincent Giammona, Lad. 5
James Giberson, Lad. 35
Ronnie Gies, Sqd. 288
Paul Gill, Eng. 54
Lt. John Ginley, Eng. 40
Jeffrey Giordano, Lad. 3
John Giordano, Hmc. 1
Keith Glascoe,

Lt. Geoffrey Guja, Bat. 43 (D)
Lt. Joseph Gullickson, Lad. 101
David Halderman, Sqd. 18
Lt. Vincent Halloran, Lad. 8
Robert Hamilton, Sqd. 41
Sean Hanley, Lad. 20 (D)
Thomas Hannafin, Lad. 5 (D)
Dana Hannon, Eng. 26
Daniel Harlin, L

Timothy Haskell, Sqd. 18 (D)
Cpt. Terence Hatton, Res. 1
Michael Haub, Lad. 4
Lt. Michael Healey, Sqd. 41
John Heffernan, Lad. 11
Ronnie Henderson, Eng. 279
Joseph Henry, Lad. 21
William Henry, Res. 1 (D)
Thomas Hetzel, L

Thomas Holohan, Eng. 6
Joseph Hunter, Sqd. 288
Cpt. Walter Hynes, Lad. 13 (D)
Jonathan Ielpi, Sqd. 288
Cpt. Frederick Ill Jr., Lad. 2
William Johnston, Eng. 6
Andrew Jordan, Lad. 132
Karl Joseph, Eng. 207
Lt. Antho Jovic, Bat.

SO BATT.00 UNIT SQD041 FF SEAN HANLEY DIV.01 BATT.02 UNIT LAD020 FF THOMAS HANNAFIN DIV.01 BATT.02 UNIT LAD

A NATION CHALLENGED: Those Who Answered the Call

BC THOMAS HASKELL JR DIV015 BATT00 UNIT DIV015 FF TIMOTHY HASKELL DIV SO BAT 00 UNIT SQD018 CPT TERENCE HATTON DIV SO BAT 00 UNIT RES001 FF MICHAEL HAUB DIV 13 BAT 00 UNIT LAD C

GRIEF IS LONGING: THAT THE CLOCK COULD BE RESET, THE TAPE OF LIFE REWOUND TO THE MOMENT BEFORE THE DEATHBLOW ~ WHEN THOSE EYES STILL SHONE, THOSE LIPS STILL BENT IN A SMILE, THAT CHEST STILL ROSE AND FELL. ✦ GRIEF IS LOVE: AN OCEAN OF IT, DROWNING ALL MEMORY OF FLAWS AND FAULTS, SWEEPING ASIDE ALL HESITATION AND RESERVATION; UNCONDITIONAL AND BOTTOMLESS. ✦ GRIEF IS GOODBYE: A LONG FAREWELL, BITTER AND HEART ~ WRENCHING, TO A LIFE LOST BEYOND RECALL, TO A WORLD THAT WILL NEVER AGAIN BE THE SAME. ✦ GRIEF IS PRIVATE: ONLY THE BEREAVED CAN TRULY KNOW THE INESCAPABLE PRISON OF ITS AGONY. ✦ THE MOST EXTRAORDINARY THING ABOUT THE AVALANCHE OF PUBLIC GRIEF THAT FOLLOWED THE HORROR WAS THAT IT WAS NOT PUBLIC IN ANY SENSE TO WHICH WE'RE ACCUSTOMED. IT WAS NOT OFFICIAL OR PRO FORMA OR ORGANIZED. WHEREVER IT CAME FROM ~ THE STREETS AND NEIGHBORHOODS OF OUR CITY, THE OTHER CITIES AND COMMUNITIES OF OUR NATION, THE OTHER NATIONS OF OUR PLANET ~ IT HAD AN INTIMATE QUALITY, AS IF EVERY ONE OF THOSE MILLIONS OF MOURNERS FELT A PERSONAL CONNECTION TO OUR FALLEN BROTHERS, WAS PERSONALLY BEREAVED BY THEIR LOSS, WAS MOVED BY AN ENTIRELY PRIVATE GRIEF....

{ 175 }

GRIEF

MICHAEL HEALEY DIV.SO BATT.00 UNIT SQD041 FF JOHN HEFFERNAN DIV.01 BATT.04 UNIT LAD011 FF RONNIE HENDERSON DIV.11 BATT.32 UNIT ENG279 FF JOSEPH HENRY DIV.01 BATT.07 UNIT LAD021

EPT FREDERICK ILL JR DIV. 03 BATT. 08 UNIT LAD 002   FF WILLIAM JOHNSTON   DIV. 01 BATT. 01 UNIT ENG 006   FF ANDRE JORDAN   DIV. 15 BATT. 38 UNIT LAD 132   FF KARL JOSEPH   DIV. 11 BATT. 31 UNIT ENG 20

An. this place could be much brighter than tomorrow.

And if you really try, you'll find there's no need to cry.

are ways to get there if you care enough for the living.

Know why there's a love that cannot lie. Love is strong,

bliss we cannot feel fear or dread. We stop existing and start living. Then it feels that always love's enough for us growing. So make a better world... And

do we keep strangling life, wound this earth, crucify its soul? Though it's plain to see this world is heavenly, be God's

glow. We could fly so high, let our spirits never die. In my heart, I feel you are all my BROTHERS. Create a world with no fear,

Heal the world", make it a better place for you and for me and the entire human race. There are people dying, if we care

Make a BETTER PLACE. Heal the world we live in, SAVE IT FOR OUR CHILDREN.

FF MANUEL MOJICA DIV.50 BATT.00 UNIT SQD 018 FF CARL MOLINARO DIV.03 BATT.08 UNIT LAD.002 FF MICHAEL MONTESI DIV.50 BATT.00 UNIT RES 001 CPT THOMAS MOODY DIV.01 BATT.99 UNIT DIV

THE BRIGHTEST SPOT IN THE SOMBER LANDSCAPE WE
NOW INHABIT IS THE CHILDREN. THEIR LITTLE SONGS OF
INNOCENCE ~ MESSAGES OF LOVE AND ADMIRATION AND
GOOD CHEER, BLURRING THE LINE BETWEEN THIS WORLD
AND THE NEXT ~ COMFORT THE GROWN~UPS, SOMEHOW
REASSURE US. THEY'RE A SWEET REMINDER THAT LIFE
ALWAYS TRIUMPHS, LIFE ALWAYS FLOWS ON, FINDING ITS
WAY AROUND THE ROCKS OF SAVAGERY AND INTOLERANCE
AND INHUMANITY.

{ 197 }

HOPE

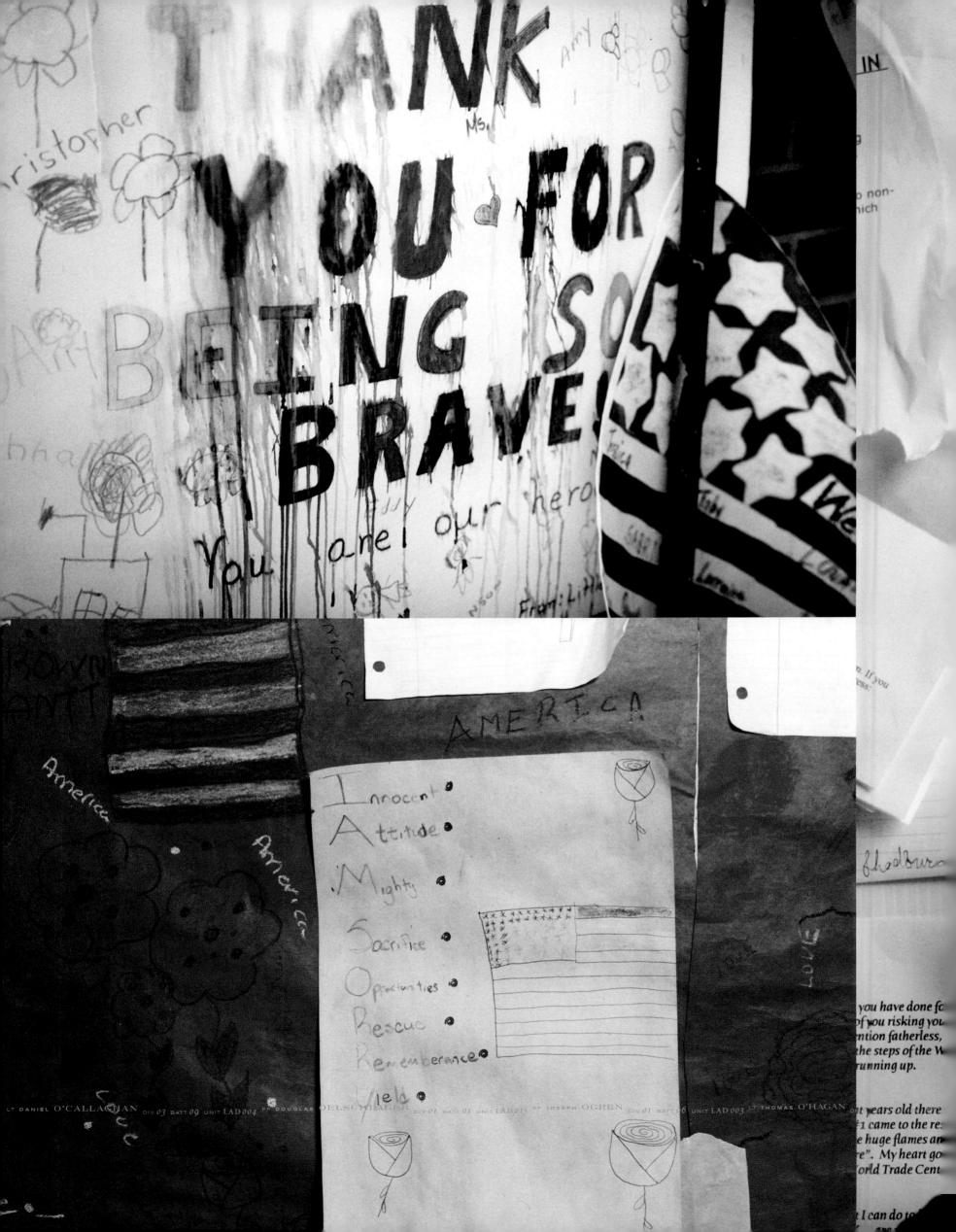

BC JOHN PAOLILLO DIV. SC BATT. SC UNIT SOC FF JAMES PAPPAGEORGE DIV. 03 BATT. 09 UNIT ENG 023 FF ROBERT PARRO DIV. 03 BATT. 08 UNIT ENG 008 FF DURRELL PEARSALL DIV. SO BATT. 00 UNIT RES

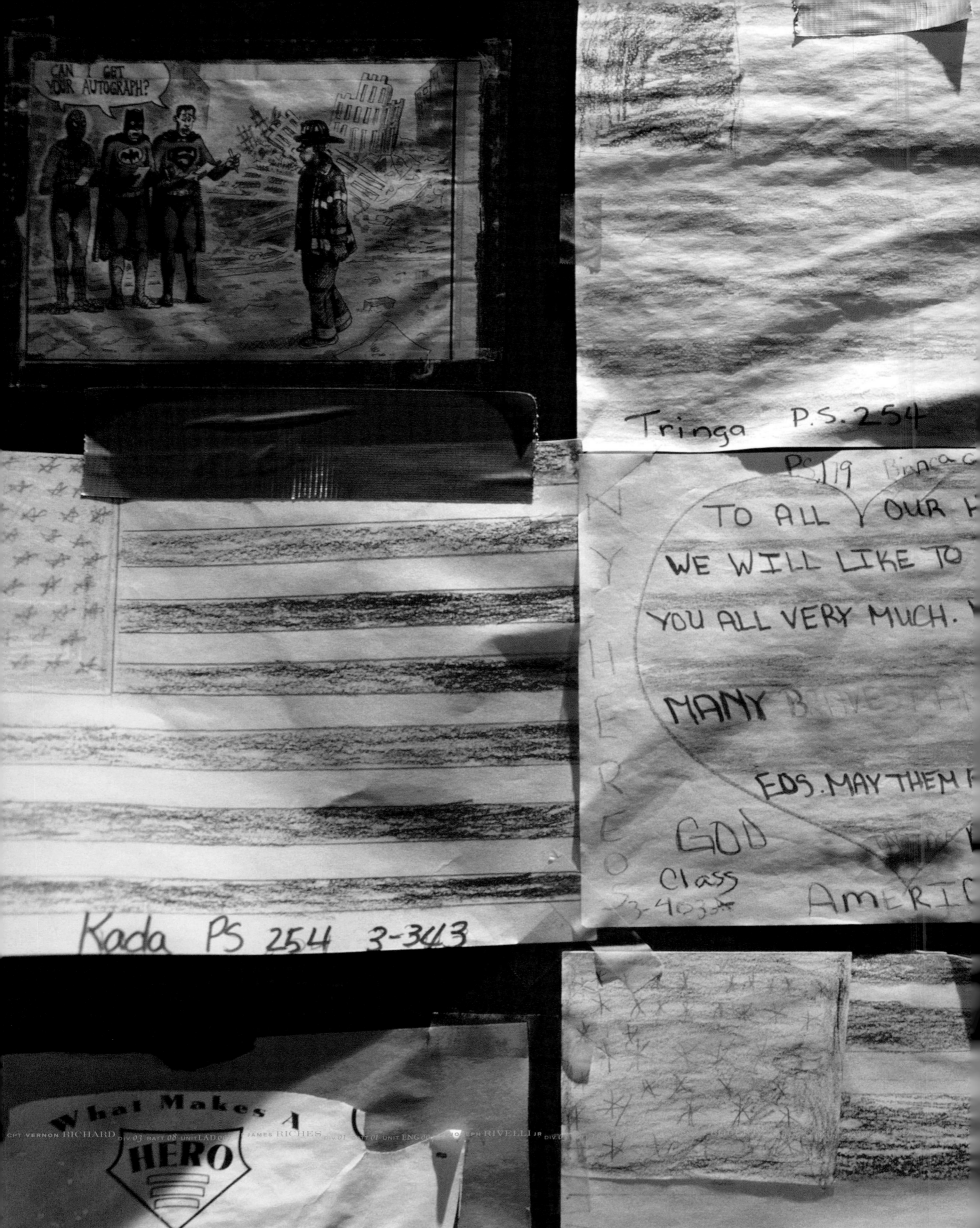

15 BATT 37 UNIT ENG 214 FF ANTHO ... UNIT ... FF MATTHEW ROGAN DIV 01 BATT 04 UNIT LAD 011 FF ... ROSSOMANDO DIV SO ... 005 FF PAUL RUBACK DIV 03 ... UNIT LAD 025

PEACE

Thank you! F.D.N.Y. Thank-you!

You guys Rock!

Arlington Heights Middle School
Clarks Summit, Pennsylvania 18411
September 19, 2001

Dear Firefighter,

   We most likely have never met, and we probably never will, so I don't know what to say to you, but, thanks.
   You may not be pulling people out of the rubble but you definatly are preventing people from falling in. So, who knows, you might be saving the life of the future President of the United States, or a big movie star, you never know do you?
   Even though I didn't loose anybody in Tuesdays tragedies I know lots of people who did. But we thank you for preventing more tragedies. I don't want to sound stupid or like I'm making this up, but you are the true heroes, and I can not expr   my

4/14/01

Dear Rescuers,
        Thank you for saving the people. I feel sad because of the firemen who hurt. Are the firemen ok? How many people did you save? Were the firefighters ok?

                                Your friend,
                                Emilio

FF JOHN SCHARDT DIV 08 BATT 40 UNIT ENG201 BC FRED SCHEFFOLD DIV 03 BATT 12 UNIT BAT012 FF THOMAS SCHOALES DIV 01 BATT 01 UNIT ENG004 FF GERARD SCHRANG DIV 50 BATT 00 UNIT RES

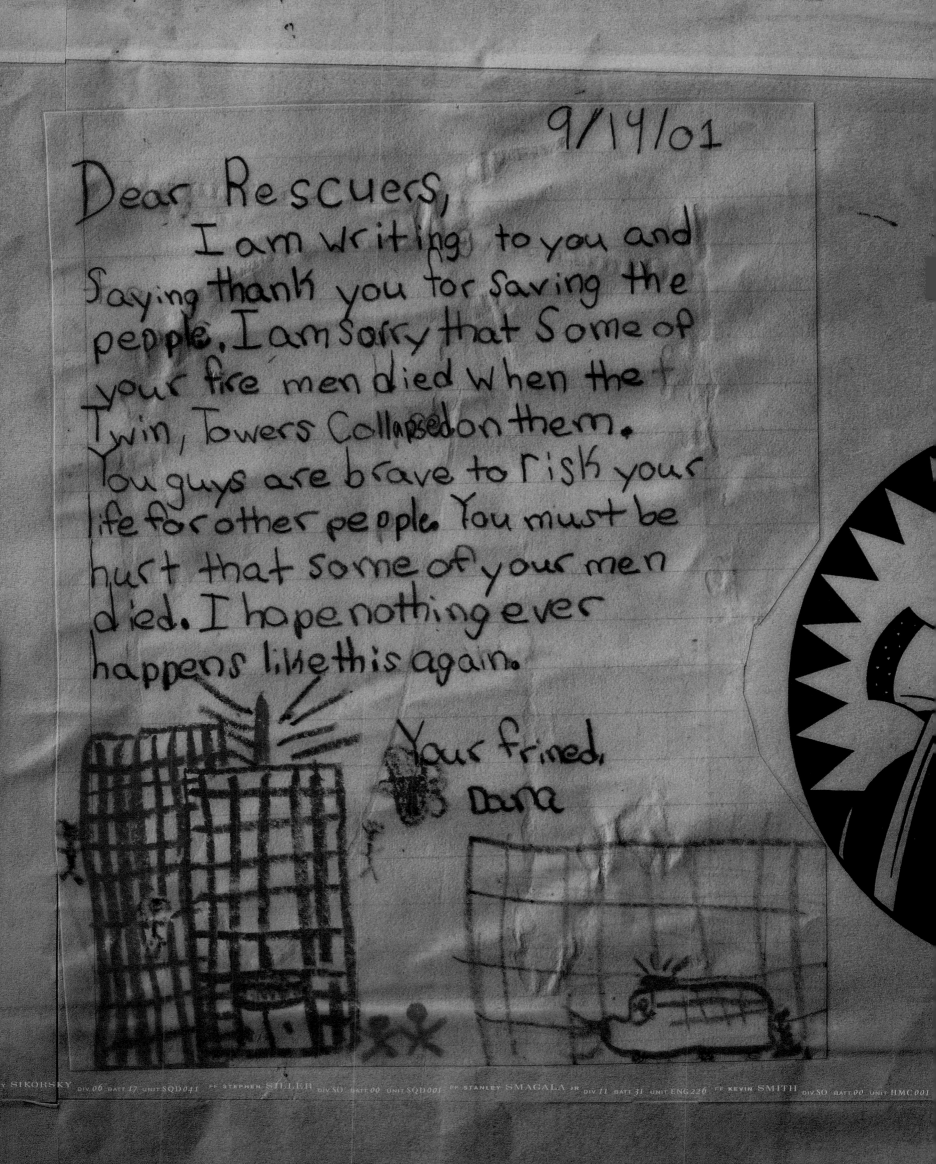

9/14/01

Dear Rescuers,
    I am writing to you and saying thank you for saving the people. I am sorry that some of your fire men died when the Twin, Towers Collapsed on them. You guys are brave to risk your life for other people. You must be hurt that some of your men died. I hope nothing ever happens like this again.

Your frined,
Dana

9/13/01

Keep hope a live

OGILVY & MATHER

Rick Boyko, Co~President, Chief Creative Officer

Michael Ian Kaye, Associate Creative Director; DESIGN ASSOCIATES: Soohyen Park, Bill Darling, Roman Luba, Spencer Bagley, Mark O'Brisky, David Goldstein

Cindy Rivet, Manager, Art Buying; Gloria Graham Hall, Associate Manager, Art Buying; Leslie D'Acri, Senior Art Buyer; ART BUYING ASSOCIATES: Maggie Sumner, Julie Boynton, Melanie Blythe

Carl Argila, Management Supervisor; Lee Roth, Account Executive

Ken Gray, Director of Operations; Joseph Burke, Director of Print Production; Kara Levens Farley, Executive Print Producer; Jeanette Luis, Print Producer; Elizabeth Kearney, Head of Traffic; TRAFFIC ASSOCIATES: Theresa Gallone, Lawrence Rossi, Sylvia Flores; Nigel Kent, Studio Manager, GSI; John Kinsella, Manager, GSI Retouching Department; GSI RETOUCHING ASSOCIATES: George Slezak, Claire Jones, Dina D'Angelo,

Franco Casas, Harumi Ando, John Davis, Randy Hiken, Russell Cook, Warren Mills, William Davis; Bob Kodadek, Manager, GSI Color; Valentin Geigel, Manager, GSI Presentation Studio; GSI STUDIO ASSOCIATES: Laurent Ohayon, Bob Perez; Michael Piper, Technology Guru; Sam Shum, Technical Support; Norm Paley, Director of Production

Karen Kassirer, Manager, Editorial Services; EDITORIAL ASSOCIATES: Tamara Armand, Marianna Najjar, John Lewis Mahoney, Frances Carlen, Christopher Caruana, Alexandra Bonfante-Warren, Kathryn Paulsen, Kathy Antrim

Jim Consolantis, Chief Integration Officer
Brian Collins, Executive Creative Director, Brand Integration Group
Michael Ward, Creative Director
Toni Lee, Public Relations Manager
Meghan Lapides, Human Resources Coordinator
Adele Farro, Executive Assistant

ACKNOWLEDGEMENTS

WE WISH TO THANK THE FOLLOWING PEOPLE AND COMPANIES FOR THEIR GENEROUS SUPPORT AND CONTRIBUTIONS.

American Express Company:

Kenneth I. Chenault, Chairman and Chief Executive Officer
John D. Hayes, Executive Vice President,
Global Advertising and Brand Management

American Express Publishing Corporation:

Ed Kelly, President and Chief Executive Officer
Mark V. Stanich, Chief Marketing Officer, Publisher
Thomas J. Fox, Vice President, Manufacturing
Judith Hill, Editor in Chief, Books
Stuart Handelman, Production Coordinator
Bruce Rosner, Vice President, Marketing
Marshall Corey, Director, Retail Sales
Elisa Shevitz, Director, Public Relations
James R. Whitney, Business Manager

The Office of the Mayor of the City of New York

The Fire Department of the City of New York

Civic Entertainment Group:

Stuart Ruderfer, David N. Cohn, Lauren Berger, Elyse Kazam

PHOTOGRAPHY AGENTS: Archard & Associates; Art & Commerce; Art Department; Bernstein & Andriulli; Brown Artist Management; Creative Management Partners; Deborah Schwartz; Edge; In Focus & Associates; i2i; Jean Conlon; Jennifer Goodin; Joan Miller; John Kenny & Associates; Judith Miller; Julian Richards; Levine & Leavitt; Magnum Photos; Marge Casey & Associates; Marzena; The Mitchell Agency; MS Logan; PMI; Proof; Susanne Bransch; Z Photographic

PHOTOGRAPHIC SERVICES: Cyclops Productions, *Mike Jurkovac;* 2D Productions, *Lisa Ilorio, Shauna Simmons, Alex Yetter*

PRE~PRESS & PRINTING SERVICES: AGT~Seven, *Gene Manning, Frank Vergone;* Central Lewmar Fine Papers; Imation Color Technologies, *Jim Metzger;* Quad/Graphics, Inc.; Sandy Alexander, *Michael Graff;* Sterling Publishing Company The Xerox Corporation, *Sean Harold*

FILM LABS: The C Lab; Chelsea B&W; Color Edge; DigiZone; Exhibition Prints; Green Rhino Inc.; LTI Photo Lab and 68 Degrees, Scott Hagendorf; U.S. Color Lab;

LEGAL SERVICES: Davis & Gilbert LLP, *Stuart Lee Friedel, Esq., Mary M. Luria, Esq.*

INDEX OF PHOTOGRAPHY

FF **JOHN** VIGIANO II DIV. *15* BATT. *38* UNIT LAD *132*   FF **SERGIO** VILLANUEVA DIV. *15* BATT. *38* UNIT LAD *132*   FF **LAWRENCE** VIRGILIO DIV. SO BATT. *00* UNIT SQD *018*   LT **ROBERT** WALLACE DIV. *11* BATT. *32* UNIT ENG *205*

FF JEFFREY WALZ DIV 01 BATT 06 UNIT LAD009   LT MICHAEL WARCHOLA   DIV 01 BATT 02 UNIT LAD005   CPT PATRICK WATERS   DIV AD BATT SO UNIT SOC   FF KENNETH WATSON   DIV 15 BATT 37 UNIT ENG214   FF MICHAEL WEINE